CHARLIE BROWN'S CYCLOPEDIA

CREATURES OF LAND AND SEA

Wild, Weird, and Wonderful

VOLUME · 4 ·

Based on the Charles M. Schulz Characters

Funk & Wagnalls

Charlie Brown's 'Cyclopedia has been produced by Mega-Books of New York, Inc. in conjunction with the editorial, design, and marketing staff of Field Publications.

STAFF FOR MEGA-BOOKS

Pat Fortunato
Editorial Director

Diana Papasergiou
Production Director

Susan Lurie
Executive Editor

Rosalind Noonan
Senior Editor

Adam Schmetterer
Research Director

Michaelis/Carpelis Design Assoc., Inc.
Art Direction and Design

STAFF FOR FIELD PUBLICATIONS

Cathryn Clark Girard
Assistant Vice President,
Juvenile Publishing

Elizabeth Isele
Executive Editor

Kristina Jones
Executive Art Director

Leslie Erskine
Marketing Manager

Elizabeth Zuraw
Senior Editor

Michele Italiano-Perla
Group Art Director

Kathleen Hughes
Senior Art Director

Photograph and Illustration credits:
Animals Animals/W. Gregory Brown, 49; Animals Animals/John Chellman, 42; Animals Animals/Bruce Davidson, 26; Animals Animals/E.R. Degginger, 46; Animals Animals/John Gerlach, 25; Animals Animals/Arthur Gloor, 45; Animals Animals/Breck P. Kent, 19, 20; Animals Animals/ Zig Leszczynski, 34, 48, 52, 55, 58; Animals Animals/Patti Murray, 29; Animals Animals/Ralph A. Reinhold, 19; Animals Animals/Stan Schroeder, 19; Animals Animals/Richard Shiell, 12; Animals Animals/Anne Wertheim, 50; David Celsi, 12, 15, 28, 29; R.A. Clevenger/West Light, 30; Bill Ross/West Light, 31.

ISBN: 0-8374-0049-X

Part of the material in this volume was previously published in *Charlie Brown's Second Super Book of Questions and Answers*.

Funk & Wagnalls, founded in 1876, is the publisher of *Funk & Wagnalls New Encyclopedia,* one of the most widely owned home and school reference sets, and many other adult and juvenile educational publications.

INTRODUCTION

Welcome to volume 4 of *Charlie Brown's 'Cyclopedia*. When we think of animals, we usually think of dogs or cats or animals in a zoo. But there are thousands of incredible sea dwellers and many insects that are wild, weird, and wonderful. Have you ever wondered what an octopus does with all those arms, or how fireflies light up, or whether electric eels really make electricity? Charlie Brown and the rest of the *Peanuts* gang are here to help you find the answers to these questions and many more. Have fun!

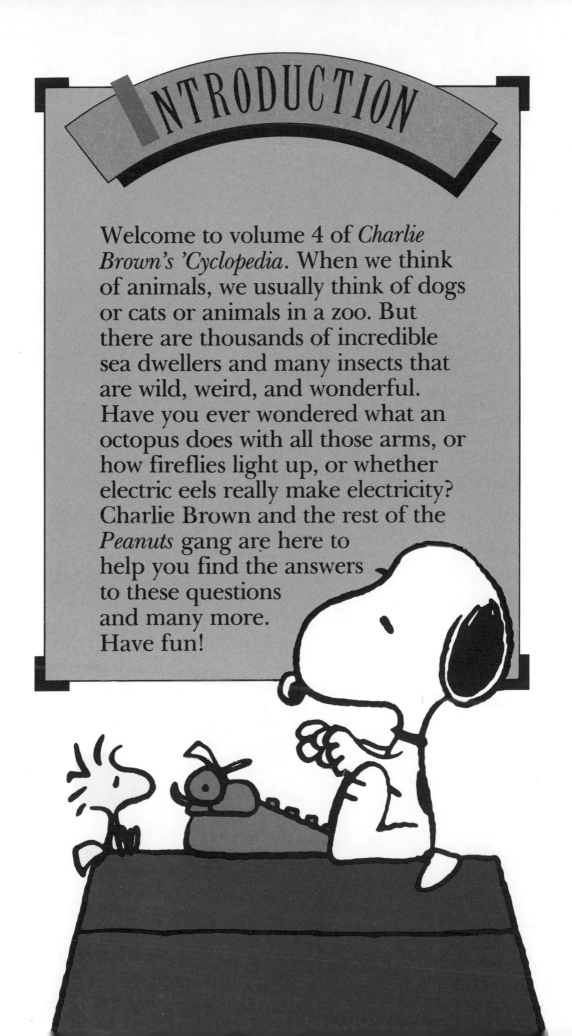

CONTENTS

Insects live almost everywhere—from the top of the highest mountains to the bottom of the driest deserts. The ocean is the only place you won't find them. Yes, our world is full of insects. In fact, they make up more than half of all living things on the Earth. But don't let that bug you!

INSECTS!

ALL ABOUT INSECTS

What is an insect?

An insect is a small animal with six legs and a body made of three parts: the head, the thorax, and the abdomen. Many insects have two feelers and four wings, but others don't. There are hundreds of thousands of different kinds of insects, and they all look a little different. Some insects are ants, bees, butterflies, termites, and roaches.

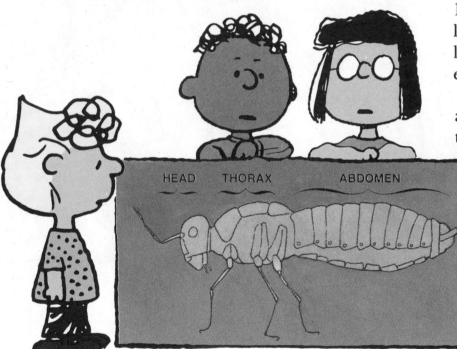

HEAD   THORAX   ABDOMEN

Where do insects come from?

They come from eggs. Female insects lay hundreds or even thousands of eggs during their lives. For example, a queen bee does nothing all summer but lay eggs. On any one day she may lay as many as 1,500. A female termite lays even more. She can lay as many as 30,000 eggs in one day!

If every insect hatched and lived its full life, the world would be overrun by them. There would be no room for anyone or anything else. Fortunately for us, many animals eat insects and insect eggs, so most insects never have a chance to grow up.

Can insects be useful to us?

We make use of insects in many ways. Bees make honey and beeswax. Silkworms make silk. An insect called the lac gives off a sticky liquid that we use to make shellac, a liquid that leaves a hard, protective finish on wood. Other insects help to get rid of harmful ones. For example, the praying mantis and the ladybug eat large numbers of harmful insects.

Bees, butterflies, moths, and other insects carry the yellow dust called pollen from flower to flower. When a flower is pollinated, the plant can grow seeds. These seeds grow to become new plants.

Are some insects harmful?

Yes. There are many harmful insects that spread disease, damage plants, and eat clothing and furniture. And there are insects, such as the mosquito, that bite us.

Ladybugs are useful insects.

Most modern dragonflies are usually 2 to 3 inches long, but some tropical species may reach 8 inches.

Why are insects so small?

Insects are small because of the way they breathe. They have no lungs for breathing air. Instead, they breathe air through tiny holes in their bodies. The air cannot travel very far through these holes. If an insect were larger, air could not reach every part of its body. The insect could not live. So, in order to get air into all parts of their bodies, insects must be relatively small.

What was the largest insect ever to live?

Many millions of years ago there lived a giant dragonfly whose body was 15 inches long. Its wings measured more than 27 inches from the tip of one wing to the tip of the opposite one. However, this insect's body was only a quarter of an inch thick. If the dragonfly had been fatter, it would not have been able to breathe.

13

Some Monarch butterflies can travel more than 2,000 miles to the south for the winter!

What is the largest insect living today?

The largest insect is a type of "walking stick" that lives in the tropics. It is very long and thin, and it looks a lot like a twig when it rests on a tree. This walking stick sometimes grows to be nearly 13 inches long.

Why are there so few insects around in the winter?

Most insects die at the end of the summer, but they leave many eggs to hatch in the spring. Bumblebees die, but they don't leave eggs. Instead, their queen stays alive all winter. She sleeps underground until spring. Then she comes out and starts laying eggs. Other insects also stay alive during the winter. These sleep underground or in a barn or cellar for the winter months. Crickets and some beetles do this. Ants do, too, but they come out on warm, sunny winter days. Monarch butterflies are like birds. They fly south to warmer places for the winter.

14

THE AMAZING ANT

What insects act most like people?

Ants do. They live in nests that are much like cities. Often the nests are built underground and are full of tunnels. They may have roads leading to and from the entrance. Inside the city, ants keep busy doing different jobs. Some clean the tunnels, some take care of babies, and some guard the city. Others go outside and gather food.

There are ants that fight wars. There are even ants that keep other insects as pets. Some kinds of ants grow their own food in gardens. Others keep ant cows.

Ants build their tunneled nests underground.

What is an ant cow?

An ant cow is another name for an insect called an aphid (AY-fid). Aphids make a sweet liquid called honeydew. Certain kinds of ants keep aphids and "milk" them, just as farmers keep cows. An ant uses its feelers to stroke an aphid's sides. The aphid then lets out a drop of honeydew for the ant to drink.

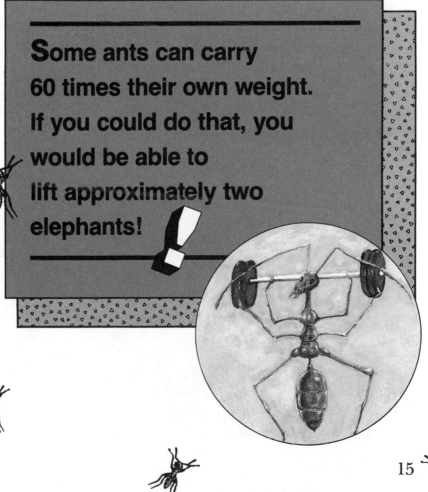

Some ants can carry 60 times their own weight. If you could do that, you would be able to lift approximately two elephants!

HONEYBEE

BEES AND WASPS

How do bees make honey?

Only one kind of bee—the honeybee —makes honey. First a honeybee goes to flowers to get nectar. Nectar is a sweet liquid found inside the flowers. A bee drinks the nectar and stores it in its "honey stomach." The honey stomach is not the same stomach that the bee uses to digest its food. It is a special stomach where the nectar is changed into watery honey.

The bee then flies back to its hive. It sucks up the watery honey from its honey stomach and places the honey in little cubbyholes called cells. In the cells, the water dries out of the honey, so the honey becomes thicker.

WASP

Why do bees buzz?

The sound of a bee buzzing is nothing more than the sound of its wings moving. So when a bee flies, you hear the buzzzzz.

Do different bees have different jobs?

Yes. Honeybees and bumblebees live in large groups called colonies and divide up the jobs that have to be done to keep the colony alive. Some bees are soldiers that must protect the hive. Other bees called workers go off to collect nectar to make honey.

One thousand bees must work their entire lives to make one pound of honey!

Why do bees sting?

Bees sting in order to protect themselves from enemies. They do not sting because they are mean. If you don't bother a bee, it will usually not feel threatened by you, and it will not sting you. However, the smell of certain perfumes may cause a bee to sting. So if you are wearing perfume and decide to take a walk outside, watch out!

Does a bee die when it stings you?

Only worker honeybees die when they sting you. No other bees do. Most of the bees that sting have smooth stingers. After one of them stings you, its stinger slips right out of your flesh. The honeybee's stinger, however, has tiny sawteeth at the end of it with a poison sack attached. As the stinger works its way through the skin, poison is also pumped into the skin. When the honeybee flies away, the stinger stays in your flesh. Soft parts of the bee's body pull off with the stinger, and the honeybee soon dies.

How dangerous is the sting of a bee or a wasp?

The sting of a bee or a wasp usually is not dangerous to people. Most of the time the sting hurts a lot, and the area around the sting swells up. After a while, though, the pain goes away, and so does the swelling. Some people, however, are allergic to the sting. They may break out in a rash, or their eyes and lips may swell up. A few people are so allergic to stings that they have trouble breathing and must quickly see a doctor. This extra-strong reaction is not common.

Three hundred babies come out of each egg laid by some wasps!

What are hornets and yellow jackets?

Hornets and yellow jackets are two of the most familiar kinds of wasps. Wasps are related to bees, and are known for their love of fruit juices and for their painful stings. Some kinds of wasps live all alone. Others, including hornets and yellow jackets, live in colonies as honeybees do. All wasps are helpful insects. The adults feed their babies insects that are harmful to people and crops.

What is a wasp's nest made of?

Different kinds of wasps make different kinds of nests. Paper wasps, including hornets and yellow jackets, build their nests of paper. They make the paper by chewing up wood. Some wasps, called mud daubers, make their nests from mud. They build rows of mud cells in protected places, such as under bridges and roofs of buildings. Potter wasps attach their mud nests to plants. These nests look like tiny clay pots! Carpenter wasps dig tunnels in wood for their nests. Digger wasps dig tunnels in the ground.

Moths, Butterflies, and the Magical Caterpillar

LUNA
MOTH

What is the difference between a moth and a butterfly?

Moths usually fly at night and butterflies fly during the day. The body of a moth is thick and hairy. The body of a butterfly is thin and not at all hairy. The feelers of a butterfly are slender and have little knobs at the ends. The moth's feelers don't have these knobs, and they are often quite feathery. Both moths and butterflies can be beautifully colored, but butterflies' colors are brighter.

MONARCH
BUTTERFLY

How does a caterpillar turn into a butterfly?

When a butterfly egg hatches, out comes a worm-like creature called a caterpillar. The caterpillar eats a lot of leaves and grows big. Then it attaches itself to a twig and grows a hard skin. Now it is called a chrysalis (KRIS-uh-lis). For weeks the chrysalis stays very still, but inside the hard covering, many changes are taking place. Four wings, six legs, feelers, and new and different eyes are forming. Finally, the covering splits open. A butterfly with tiny, damp wings comes out. It hangs on a twig until its wings dry out. Then it is ready to fly away.

MONARCH
CATERPILLAR

Inside this cocoon, a caterpillar is changing into a moth.

Do butterflies spin cocoons?

No, but moths do. When a moth caterpillar is big enough, it spins a protective case around itself. This case is called a cocoon. The cocoon is spun of silk threads, which the caterpillar makes in its body. The caterpillar rests inside its cocoon and slowly changes into a moth. Like the butterfly, the moth comes out of its covering and flies away.

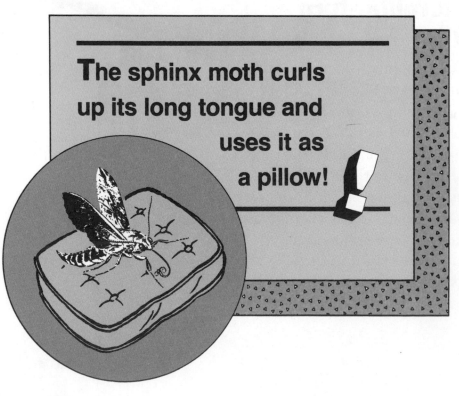

The sphinx moth curls up its long tongue and uses it as a pillow!

How do we get silk from silkworms?

The silkworm is really a caterpillar that will someday become a small moth. It spins a cocoon of silk just as other moth caterpillars do, but its silk is especially fine.

The silkworm's silk comes out of its mouth as a thread of gluey liquid. The thread hardens as soon as it touches the air. The thread is often as long as 1,000 feet! The caterpillar winds the thread around and around its body to form a cocoon.

To get the silk, people heat the cocoon and kill the caterpillar inside. Next they put the cocoon in warm water to soften the gum that holds the threads in place. Then they can unwind the thread. From the thread, fine silk material is woven.

Why do moths gather around light bulbs at night?

Many insects are attracted to light. They have an instinct to go toward it. A moth is one of these insects. When a light goes on, a moth is drawn to it. The moth can't stay away. Since moths are awake at night, you will often see a group of them flying round and round a light bulb.

Why do moths eat your clothes?

Actually, grown moths don't eat your clothes. Certain moth *caterpillars* eat them. Rugs and clothes are their favorite foods. They especially like wool and fur. These caterpillars get into your closet or drawer if a female moth lays her eggs there. When the eggs hatch, the hungry little caterpillars come out and go to work on your clothes.

SUPER PESTS: FLIES, TERMITES, MOSQUITOES, AND ROACHES

Why are house flies super pests?

Flies are super pests because they can carry bacteria that can make us sick. So we swat them away when they crawl on food—or on us!

How can a fly walk on the ceiling?

A fly can walk upside-down on the ceiling because of the pads on each of its six feet. If you look at a fly with a magnifying glass, you can see these pads clearly. Some scientists think that the fly stays on the ceiling because the pads are sticky. Others believe that the curved pads flatten out against the ceiling and hold on the way suction cups do.

How do worms get into apples?

GOOD GRIEF. THERE WAS A WORM IN MY APPLE!

They are born there! But they're not really worms. They're one stage in the life of insects such as codling moths and fruit flies. For example, in the middle of summer, when apples are growing on apple trees, female fruit flies push their eggs inside some of the apples. The inside of an apple is the perfect place for a young fly because it is moist, protected, and surrounded by food. The eggs hatch into tiny wormlike creatures called larvae (LAR-vee). If no one picks the apples, they fall off the trees in the autumn. The larvae crawl out and bury themselves in the ground. A hard skin forms around each one. Then next summer, a fly comes out of the skin.

Why do termites eat the frames of our houses?

Termites eat wooden house frames because wood is their favorite food—and because wood houses make a perfect home for termites. Termites chew holes that they use as rooms to live in. They line the tunnels and holes with chewed-up wood that they have made into a kind of clay.

Wood-eating termites damage more than the frames of houses. They eat wooden bridges, fences, and boats. In certain countries that are always warm, termites may get *inside* houses and eat furniture, books, and paper. Look what termites did to Snoopy's house!

How do termites digest wood?

Termites get help from tiny creatures called protozoa (pro-tuh-ZOE-uh). Thousands of these one-celled animals live inside each termite. The termite eats wood, and the protozoa digest the wood. The termite is then able to digest what they leave behind. The protozoa and termite are a team. They need each other. In fact, they couldn't survive without each other. When two creatures depend on each other in this way, we call their relationship symbiosis (sim-by-OH-sis).

TERMITES CAN BE SO NOISY!

CHOMP CHOMP CHOMP

Do all mosquitoes bite?

No, only female mosquitoes bite. When one bites you, she pricks your skin with a long, thin part of her mouth. Then she sucks some of your blood for food. The mosquito has a special liquid in her mouth to keep your blood thin and easy to suck. Some of this liquid gets under your skin. It causes the bite to swell and itch because most people are allergic to this liquid. However, there are a few people who are not allergic and don't itch at all from mosquito bites!

Will we ever get rid of cockroaches?

Cockroaches are experts at staying alive. They have been around since the days of the dinosaur—many millions of years! Cockroaches can eat almost anything— garbage, soap, book bindings, even television wires! People kill cockroaches with poisons, but cockroach babies are often born immune to the same poison that killed their parents. This means that the babies cannot be killed by that poison, and something new has to be found to do the job.

Cockroaches do not bite, and they usually don't spread disease, but no one wants to have them around. They like damp and dirty places, and places like kitchens where they're likely to find food. So a clean, dry house may discourage them from coming in. But they'll probably still be living out there for the next million years!

WHAT'S IN A NAME?

DARNING NEEDLE

Do darning needles sew?

From their name it sounds as if they might—and they look as if they might—but they don't. The darning needle's real name is dragonfly. Dragonflies are scary-looking insects, but they are really perfectly harmless. In fact, darning needles are very helpful to us. They eat many insect pests, such as flies and mosquitoes.

Does a doodlebug like to doodle?

No. Doodlebug is just another name for a young ant lion. An ant lion is not an ant and it's not a lion. It is an insect that—to an ant—might seem as ferocious as a lion seems to us.

In the early part of its life, an ant lion digs a pit in sand and buries itself at the bottom. Only its head sticks out. It waits for an ant to fall into the pit. When one does, the ant lion then kills it with its big jaws and sucks the juices out of its body.

A dragonfly can keep up with a car moving 50 miles an hour!

25

In some foreign countries, people tie praying mantises to their beds to catch pesky insects!

How did the praying mantis get its name?

When a praying mantis holds its front legs up together, it looks as if it is praying. However, this insect is not praying at all. It is waiting for a smaller insect to come by so that it can grab the insect with its front legs. The praying mantis will crush the insect and eat it. People like the praying mantis because it eats many insects that harm our crops.

What is the "fire" in the firefly?

Fireflies make two special juices in their bodies. When these juices mix together, fireflies light up. Scientists are not sure why fireflies make this light, but they think that a firefly's glow is probably a signal to attract a mate.

CHAPTER 2

Did you know that spiders are not insects? They belong to the group of animals called arachnids (uh-RAK-nids). This group includes lots of creatures such as scorpions, mites, ticks, and daddy longlegs, too. What's so special about spiders and their crawling relatives? Let's find out!

SPIDERS AND OTHER CRAWLING THINGS

ALL ABOUT SPIDERS

What's the difference between spiders and insects?

Insects have six legs, and spiders have eight. An insect's body has three main parts. A spider's body has only two. Most insects have feelers and wings. Spiders don't have either.

Are spiders dangerous to people?

Not many spiders are dangerous. Most spiders are harmless to people. In fact, they're very helpful because they eat flies, mosquitoes, ants, and other insect pests.

What happens to spiders in the winter?

Most spiders die when winter begins, but they leave their eggs behind so that baby spiders will be born in the spring. Wolf spiders live longer, usually from 6 to 7 years. Some tarantulas have been known to live for 20 years.

SPIDERS AND THEIR WEBS

How does a spider spin a web?

A spider spins a web out of silk that it makes inside its body. The silk comes out in very thin liquid threads. As soon as a thread touches the air, it hardens. Some of the threads are sticky and some are not. The spider attaches the threads to a tree or house in a particular pattern. One kind of web you may have seen is called an orb web. It looks something like a wheel. Insects get caught in the sticky threads of the "wheel." The spider then kills the insects and eats them.

Do all kinds of spiders spin webs?

No, they don't. Many lie in wait for their prey and then pounce on it. The trap-door spider builds a door that opens into a hole in the ground. It then waits inside for an insect to walk by and fall in.

If you strung a pound of spiders' threads end to end, they would circle the Earth!

ORB WEAVER SPIDER

Why aren't spiders caught in their own webs?

A spider is careful to walk only on the nonsticky threads of its web. Even if it does slip and touch the sticky threads, it isn't caught. It is protected by an oily covering on its body.

BLACK WIDOWS AND TARANTULAS

Is the bite of a black widow spider very dangerous?

Yes, it is. But there aren't many cases reported, and there are medicines to treat people who have been bitten.

The full-grown female black widow is the kind that is dangerous. You can recognize it easily because it is shiny black and has a red hourglass-shaped mark on its underside.

Aren't tarantulas dangerous, too?

The tarantula isn't deadly, though it's very big and looks fierce. Its bite is painful, but it doesn't really make a person sick.

:WHEW!:

POISONOUS BLACK WIDOW SPIDER

DADDY LONGLEGS, SCORPIONS, MITES, AND TICKS

What is a daddy longlegs?

A daddy longlegs is a close relative of the spider, but it does not spin a web. You can easily recognize a daddy longlegs by its tiny body and eight very long, skinny legs. If it loses one of its legs, it will grow a new one! Daddy longlegs don't catch live insects. They eat mainly leaves and grass and insects that are already dead.

Can a scorpion's sting kill you?

Most scorpions aren't really dangerous. Only the large scorpions living in the South have a poisonous sting, powerful enough to make a person very sick.

SCORPION

What are mites and ticks?

Mites are tiny, spiderlike animals that feed mainly on fruits, flowers, and other plant leaves. Some, such as the scabies mite, feed on the skin of people.

Ticks are also very small, but they can carry serious diseases, such as Lyme disease, from animals to people. If a tick sucks the blood of an infected animal and then moves to a person, it can transfer the infection. It's not hard to protect yourself against ticks. When going into the woods, cover your arms and legs, and spray your clothing with a tick repellent. Then when you get home, check your body and clothing for ticks.

31

There's a living world of wonderful shapes and colors under the sea. Let's go to the ocean floor and visit the creatures that live there. As you read on, Charlie Brown will take you on an exciting underwater adventure!

SOMETHING FISHY

FACTS ABOUT FISH

What is a fish?

A fish is an animal that lives in water and has bones inside its body. Fish are cold-blooded, which means that their body temperature is the same as the water temperature. Almost all fish have fins, which help them swim, and most have scales to protect their bodies.

How many kinds of fish are there?

Altogether there are about 21,000 kinds of fish. We divide these into three main groups. One small group, called lamprey eels, has no jaws at all and suck in food with just their mouths. The second group is very old. These fish don't have real bones inside them but only cartilage (CAR-til-luj), which is softer than bone. This group includes sharks. The third and largest group of fish all have bones inside their bodies. Goldfish, bullheads, and tuna are some of the fish in this group.

Different fish can look amazingly different. Fish are every color you can imagine—red, green, gray, yellow, purple, orange, blue, and brown. Some have stripes, some have spots, others have fancy patterns. Fish vary in size and shape from short and fat to long and thin.

Panel 1: DOGS LIKE TO BE SCRATCHED BEHIND THEIR EARS, DON'T THEY?

Panel 2: OF COURSE, YOU CAN'T EXPECT ME TO DO IT FOREVER..

Panel 3: YOU COULD AT LEAST KEEP DOING IT UNTIL YOUR ARMS FALL OFF...

Can any fish live out of water?

Yes, a few fish can live out of water—some for hours, some for days, and some for years! Mudskippers hop around on land and even climb trees. So do climbing perch. Walking catfish can crawl along the ground and breathe air for a few days at a time. How do they do it? They have a special chamber in their gills to help them breathe.

Some fish have gills—and lungs, too! Its lungs help the lungfish spend a lot of time on land. In summer, the streams where it lives often dry up. So the lungfish curls up in a ball of mud at the bottom of a stream. It may sleep there for months—or even for years—until the rains come again. While it is sleeping, the lungfish breathes air through a little hole it has made in the mudball.

How can fish breathe in water?

Fish can breathe in water because of the way their bodies are made. Fish need to breathe the gas called oxygen in order to live. Oxygen is in the air and in the water, too. Land animals have lungs, which can take oxygen from air but not from water. Fish don't have lungs. They have gills. Gills can take oxygen from water.

When a fish breathes, it takes water in through its mouth. The water flows through the gills, which take oxygen out of it. Then the water goes out of the fish's body through openings behind the gills.

MUDSKIPPERS

Can fish live in a frozen pond?

If the pond is frozen solid from top to bottom, then fish *cannot* live there. Solid ice will not give fish the oxygen they need to keep alive. But usually when we talk about a frozen pond, we mean one with just a covering of ice. This sheet of ice has water below it, where fish can live. They usually stay near the bottom of the pond, where the temperature is warmer.

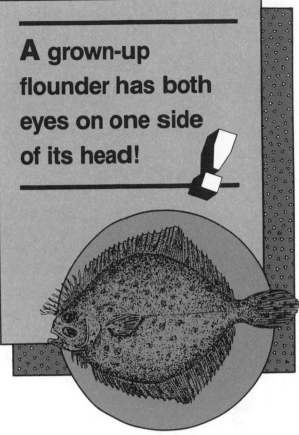

A grown-up flounder has both eyes on one side of its head!

Do fish sleep?

Most fish do sleep—but with their eyes open! Fish cannot close their eyes, because they have no eyelids. When sleeping, many fish lie on their side or belly at the bottom of the pond, river, ocean, or aquarium where they live. The fish that don't sleep take rests. They just stop swimming and stay in one place for a while.

35

What do fish eat?

Because so many other water creatures are looking for food, too, most fish eat just about anything they can get. They eat insects, worms, and water animals, including other fish. Some even eat their own babies. There are fish that eat plants, too, but not many eat just plants.

Can fish make sounds?

A few can. A fish called the croaker makes a deep, grumpy-sounding *gur-rumph*. The sound is made in the fish's belly and is a lot like the noise a bull-frog makes. The grunting catfish makes a sound, too—but only when you take it out of water.

Does a fish feel pain when caught on a hook?

A hooked fish probably feels very little pain. In order for any animal to feel pain, it must have many nerves in the area that is hurt. The nerves send a message of pain to the animal's brain. A fish has very few nerves in its mouth, where it usually gets hooked. So it cannot feel very much there.

What fish is the smallest?

The pygmy goby is the smallest adult fish. It hardly ever grows longer than one-third of an inch, which is only this long: ____.

Which fish is the biggest?

The whale shark is the biggest fish. It can grow up to 59 feet long, and it can weigh up to 15 tons—more than twice as much as an African elephant! Fortunately for the other fish, the whale shark eats only plankton (PLANK-tun). Plankton is made of tiny, tiny bits of living matter that float in the sea.

WHALE SHARK

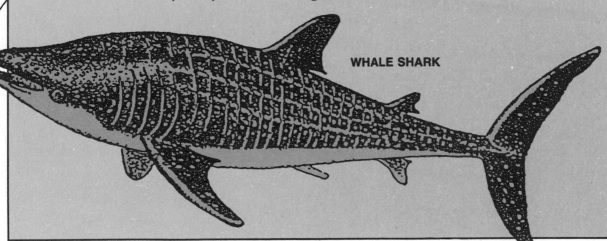

SUPER SWIMMERS

Do all fish swim?

One kind of fish does not swim. It walks along the sand at the bottom of the water. This is the batfish. The batfish lives in shallow saltwater. Its fins are not really fins—they are more like legs. The batfish uses them to walk around.

The upside-down catfish swims on its back!

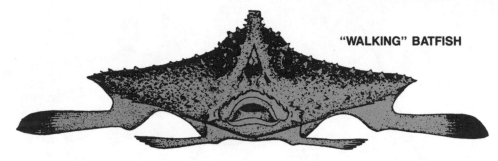

"WALKING" BATFISH

How fast can fish swim?

The fastest fish is the sailfish, which sometimes swims at more than 60 miles an hour. A few fish can swim between 30 and 45 miles an hour. Most are much slower. A small trout moves along at only 4 miles an hour, but it still swims faster than you do!

"SPEEDING" SAILFISH

What is a school of fish?

A school of fish is not a classroom. Fish schools are groups of fish that stay together. In a school, fish have more protection against hungry enemies. Each school is made up of only one kind of fish. You will never find bluefish and herring together in the same school. Nor will you ever even find baby fish in the same school as adult fish.

How many fish are in a school?

The number of fish in one school can vary. You might find twenty-five in a school of tuna—or hundreds of millions in a school of sardines.

Sharks and Piranhas

SHARK

Are sharks dangerous?

Yes, many of them are dangerous, but some small ones aren't. The great white shark is especially dangerous. This shark has made many attacks on humans, mostly in Australia. It is strange to think that sharks have no real bones inside but often have terrible jaws and teeth. Even a shark's skin is dangerous. It is covered with tiny sharp spines that are like little teeth. You can get hurt just brushing against a shark.

I WOULDN'T WORRY, MARCIE. PIRANHAS LIVE ONLY IN THE AMAZON.

Is any fish more dangerous than a shark?

Some people think that the piranha (pih-RAHN-yuh) might be more dangerous than a shark. Although piranhas are small, they have very sharp teeth. These fish travel in schools of thousands and attack all at once. In just a few minutes, a school of piranhas can eat all the flesh off a big fish or off an animal that falls into the water. Piranhas live in only one region—the Amazon of South America.

SEA SERPENTS AND ELECTRIC EELS

Are there any sea serpents?

Yes, there are, but they are not monsters. They are simply snakes that live in the sea or fish that have snakelike bodies. One of these fish is the oarfish. It grows to be 25 or 30 feet long and has bright red spines sticking out of its head. It looks pretty frightening, but is really quite harmless.

What do baby eels look like?

Baby eels don't look at all like their parents. They look like tiny glass leaves. As they grow, they change into the long, thin fish we recognize as eels.

Does an electric eel really make electricity?

Yes, it does. This fish's body is something like a car battery. It makes and stores electricity, which the eel can turn on and off. An electric eel uses the electricity in its body to catch food and to scare off enemies. The shock the eel gives can be strong enough to throw a man across a room. Small water animals are stunned by the shock and can't get away from the hungry eel. Scientists are still trying to find out exactly how this fish makes its electricity.

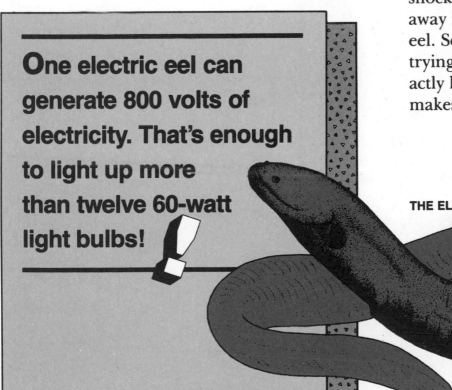

One electric eel can generate 800 volts of electricity. That's enough to light up more than twelve 60-watt light bulbs!

THE ELECTRIC EEL

41

FLYING FISH, GOLDFISH, SEA HORSES, AND MERMAIDS

FLYING FISH

GOLDFISH

Do flying fish really fly?

No, flying fish do not really fly. They glide through the air. Flying would mean that they flapped their fins the way a bird flaps its wings, but these fish don't move their fins when they are out of the water. They simply spread wide their large fins and sail through the air at great speed. Flying fish glide above the water in order to escape from their enemies, which are mostly dolphins.

When a flying fish wants to glide, it swims very quickly to the top of the water. As its head comes out of the water, the fish gives a powerful flip of its tail. This pushes the fish into the air. It can glide above the sea for up to 300 yards at a time.

In a large pond, a goldfish can grow to be as long as your arm!

How long can goldfish live?

At least one goldfish is known to have lived 40 years. Most goldfish can live about 17 years. Pet goldfish in aquariums don't usually live that long. They often die young from dirty water or a sudden change in water temperature.

Is a sea horse a fish?

Yes, a sea horse is a fish, even though it doesn't look much like one. Except for its head, it doesn't look much like a horse, either. A sea horse doesn't move the way most fish do. It swims in an upright position, with its head up and its tail pointing down. The one fin on its back moves very quickly and pushes the sea horse along in the water.

What is a mermaid?

The word *mermaid* means sea maiden. Mermaids are supposed to be beautiful sea creatures who are half human and half fish. But they exist only in fairy tales. Legend says that Christopher Columbus thought he saw a mermaid while on a voyage in the Atlantic Ocean! What he probably saw was a manatee, or sea cow, a huge sea creature with two flippers and a spoon-shaped tail. Some people say its form somewhat resembles a mermaid's.

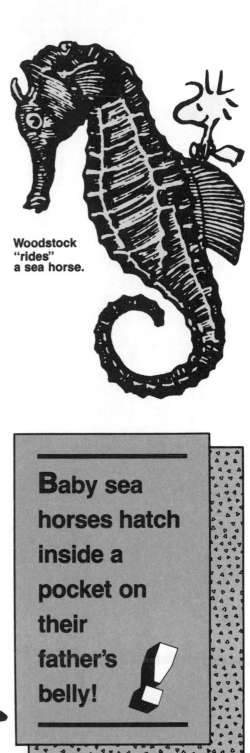

Woodstock "rides" a sea horse.

SWIMMING MY WAY, SWEETIE?

Baby sea horses hatch inside a pocket on their father's belly!

43

Let's take a walk along the sand and surf and visit some other unusual creatures that live there. What makes some of these animals of the sea so special? Well, it's not what they have. It's what they don't have. They don't have bones!

NO BONES ABOUT IT

ANIMALS THAT LIVE IN SHELLS

What are seashells?

Seashells are the hard, protective cases that certain sea animals form around themselves. Oysters, mussels, clams, scallops, and snails are some animals that have shells.

Usually, the shells are empty by the time you spot them on the seashore. The animals have been eaten by other sea animals or by sea gulls. The shells are often pretty, and it's fun to collect them.

SNAIL

How do snails walk?

Snails, like most shellfish, have no legs. But most shellfish have a foot. The whole bottom part of a snail's body is one smooth, flat foot. The snail pushes its foot out from under its shell and pulls itself along a surface. As the snail moves, its foot gives off a liquid. This liquid helps the snail move more easily.

Can you really hear the sea in a seashell?

No, you can't. When you hold a large spiral-shaped shell to your ear, you hear a roar. But it's not the roar of the sea. The shape of the shell makes any slight sound in the air echo back and forth inside the shell. Sounds that you normally hear are picked up by the shell and made louder.

The shell of a giant clam may weigh up to 600 pounds!

45

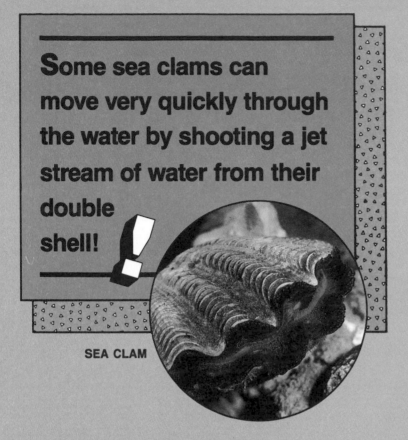

Some sea clams can move very quickly through the water by shooting a jet stream of water from their double shell!

SEA CLAM

Can a crab grow new parts if a piece of its body is cut off?

Yes. If you pick up a crab by one leg, it may let its leg drop off in order to escape. It then grows a new leg. Some crabs grow more than one new leg, which explains why fishermen often catch crabs with extra legs.

ROCK CRAB

How does an oyster make a pearl?

Sometimes a little grain of sand gets inside the shell of a pearl oyster. The sand rubs against the soft body of the oyster. To stop the rubbing, the oyster wraps the sand in layer after layer of the same shiny coating it makes to line its shell. We call this coating "mother-of-pearl." Gradually the bit of sand is wrapped in so many layers that a little ball forms. This ball is a pearl. Today, many of the pearls that are sold are produced by raising oysters and deliberately putting a bead inside the shell. This causes the oyster to make a pearl around it. We call these pearls "cultured."

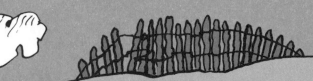

What is a horseshoe crab?

The horseshoe crab isn't a crab at all. It's much more closely related to a spider. With a shiny shell as big as a man's helmet and lots of skinny legs underneath, the horseshoe crab looks fierce. But it's really quite harmless. Horseshoe crabs have been on the Earth for millions of years.

HORSESHOE CRAB

What is a hermit crab?

A hermit crab is born without a hard shell. Because it doesn't have a shell of its own, it has to find a shell from another animal that will fit. The shell becomes the crab's home and protects it from its enemies. When it outgrows the shell, the crab has to find a new home, a larger shell from another animal.

What are barnacles?

Barnacles are a kind of shellfish that spend their adult lives fastened to one spot. Some attach themselves to rocks. Others cling to crabs, whales, sharks, and ships. One ship can be the home for more than 100 tons of barnacles! Sometimes barnacles have to be scraped off ship bottoms because their weight and roughness slow the ship's speed.

THE AMAZING OCTOPUS

Is an octopus a fish?

No. An octopus lives in the sea, but it is more closely related to clams and other shellfish than it is to real fish.

Why does an octopus squirt black ink into the water?

An octopus squirts black ink in order to cloud the water. Then the octopus can hide from an enemy. That enemy may be a shark, a whale, or a person.

What does an octopus do with its eight arms?

An octopus uses its eight arms to catch crabs, clams, lobsters, and other shellfish. It also uses its arms to break open the shells of shellfish so it can eat them. On the underside of each arm are round muscles that act like suction cups. These can hold on to anything the octopus catches.

OCTOPUS

MORE BONELESS WONDERS

Is a sponge really an animal?

Yes. It is an ancient animal that lives in the sea. This animal has no legs, arms, fins, or stomach, and it doesn't move around at all. But each sponge has lots of tiny holes called pores. As water passes through these holes, the sponge takes out food particles. That's why sponges are sometimes called the filter of the sea.

A sponge can hold a lot of water, so people have long used sponges for cleaning. Real, natural sponges are still used for some kinds of work, but today, the sponge you use to wipe up a spill was probably made in a factory.

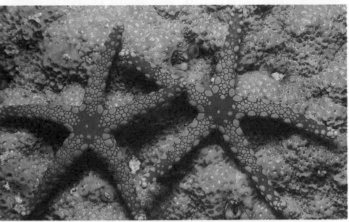

STARFISH

What is a starfish?

A starfish is a sea creature shaped like a star. Most starfish have five arms. They come in incredible colors—red, blue, even hot pink! If you cut a starfish into pieces, each piece will grow into a new starfish.

The basket starfish has more than 80,000 arms!

What sea animal looks like a flower?

The sea anemone (uh-NEM-uh-nee) looks like a flower, or at least like some sort of plant. It is a very simple animal—just a hollow tube with a mouth at one end and a lot of wavy "arms" around the mouth. The arms are used to capture food. Sea anemones come in a variety of colors—red, green, brown, and orange. Some have dots and some have stripes.

SEA ANEMONE

Can you eat a sea cucumber?

Yes, but it doesn't taste like the cucumber grown in a garden. In fact, a sea cucumber isn't a vegetable at all. It's an animal that lives at the bottom of the sea. We call it a sea cucumber because it is long and thin and looks like a cucumber. Although you won't find these cucumbers in a salad, you can eat them at some Chinese restaurants.

What is a jellyfish?

A jellyfish is a sea animal with a soft body and no shell. Some jellyfish are made up of several animals with different shapes that swim together and act like one creature. The Portuguese man-of-war is such a creature. If you meet a jellyfish in the ocean, you'll recognize it. It looks just like jelly!

Why do jellyfish sting?

Jellyfish sting in order to get food. First the jellyfish paralyzes a small animal with its sting. Because the animal then cannot move, the jellyfish can grab it and eat it. When you are swimming in the ocean, you may bump into a jellyfish and get stung. The sting may hurt, but you won't be paralyzed. So don't worry—the jellyfish will never eat *you*!

CHAPTER 5

Are they super spies or secret agents? Not these animals. But they live on land *and* in the water, so we say they have double lives. They are called amphibians.

ANIMALS WITH DOUBLE LIVES

FANTASTIC AMPHIBIANS

What are amphibians?

Amphibians (am-FIB-ee-uns) are animals that are born with gills for breathing in water, just like fish. Later, most of them develop lungs for breathing air. Most live in the water when they are young. After they have grown up they live on land, although they return to the water to mate and lay eggs. Like fish, amphibians are cold-blooded. When an animal is cold-blooded, its body has the same temperature as the air or water around it.

The amphibians include frogs, toads, salamanders, and caecilians (see-SIL-ee-unz). Caecilians are blind, wormlike animals that live underground when grown.

FROGS

What is a tadpole?

A tadpole is a baby frog or a baby toad, but it looks more like a fish. Tadpoles have no legs, and they have long tails. They breathe through gills the way fish do.

Where does the tadpole's tail go when the tadpole becomes a frog?

As a tadpole changes into a frog, its tail seems to get smaller and smaller. But the tail is not really shrinking. It is changing. It is slowly becoming part of the rest of the tadpole's body. During this time of change, the tadpole grows legs. Its gills change into lungs so it can breathe air.

What do frogs eat?

Luckily for us, frogs eat mosquitoes. They also eat flies, moths, beetles, small crayfish, and worms. A frog's mouth is very large. It has two rows of teeth on the upper jaw and none on the lower jaw. A frog has a long sticky tongue attached to the front, not the back, of its mouth. This tongue can be flicked out quickly to catch insects.

What is the world's largest frog?

The largest frog is the Goliath frog of West Africa. The biggest one ever caught weighed more than seven pounds and was more than 32 inches long with its legs spread out behind it.

The world's smallest frog could fit inside a thimble!

Do people really eat frogs' legs?

Yes, many people enjoy eating frogs' legs. The large hind legs—the jumping legs—are the ones eaten. They are usually cooked in butter. Many restaurants have frogs' legs on the menu. Frogs are even raised on frog farms to supply the demand for this unusual dish.

How far can a frog jump?

The longest frog jump on record is 17 feet and 4 inches.

TOADS

What's the difference between a frog and a toad?

A toad is usually a chubby creature with rough, bumpy skin and no teeth. A frog is thinner, has smooth skin, and usually has teeth. Like all amphibians, frogs and toads are born in the water and return there to mate. Many frogs, however, also spend a large part of their adult lives in the water, while most toads do not. A frog's eggs are often found in big clumps in the water. A toad's eggs are often found in long strings, like beads.

FROG

TOAD

Can you get warts from a toad?

No, you cannot get warts by touching a toad. That is just super-stition. The rough skin of a toad looks as if it is covered with warts, and that is probably why the story got started.

However, the toad is not completely harm-less. When a toad is at-tacked, it sends out a liquid poison from the bumps on its skin. The poison hurts the at-tacker's mouth and may keep it from eating the toad. If you catch a toad, and it lets out some of this liquid, be careful not to rub your eyes. The liquid will make them sore.

A toad eats about 100 insects every day!

SALAMANDERS

What is the biggest amphibian?

The world's largest amphibian is the giant salamander of China and Japan. One found in 1920 was 5 feet long and weighed almost 100 pounds.

Where do salamanders live?

Adult salamanders are never far from water. They die if they can't keep their skin moist. Some grown salamanders live in ponds and streams. Others live on land, in damp places that are cool and dark. You can find them in shady woods. Often they lie under stones or in hollow logs.

What are mud puppies, newts, and efts?

Mud puppies and newts are simply kinds of salamanders. During the time newts are living on land, they are called efts. As efts, they are orange colored. When they go back to water to mate, they turn green.

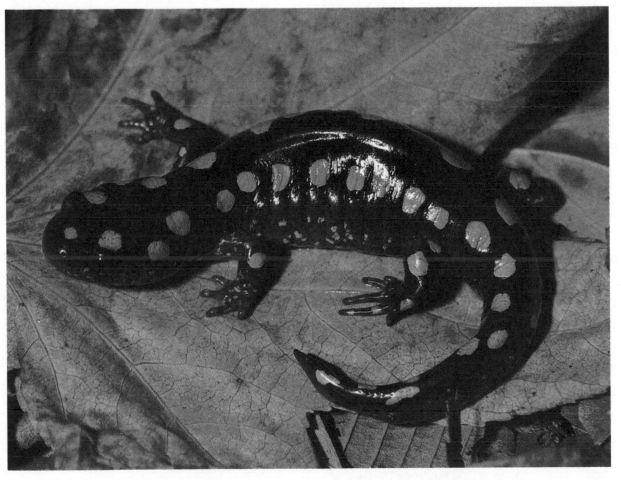

SALAMANDER

• Camouflage (KA-muh-flodge), blending in with your surroundings, can be very important in the animal world. The inchworm is a real camouflage artist. When an enemy such as a bird comes near, the inchworm freezes and pretends to be a twig. It blends in so well that the bird will often walk right across the "twig" and miss its lunch.

• Crickets don't use their mouths or throats to make their chirping sound. They rub their wings together. Only male crickets make this sound. They attract female crickets with it.

• The amazing earthworm doesn't have to worry when it gets cut in two. The pieces will wiggle around for a while, then the smaller piece usually dies. The larger piece often grows back the sections it lost—if it lost just a few. This is possible because an earthworm's body is made up of a long row of sections that are all pretty much the same. When a few sections are cut away, the worm can replace them.

• The longest earthworm ever found was nine feet long! It was found in Australia.

• The leafy seadragon looks more like a plant than a fish. Its body and fins look like branches of seaweed. It lives in the ocean off the coast of Australia.

- The giant Goliath beetle of Africa is the heaviest insect. It weighs almost four ounces, about as much as a box of 16 crayons. Despite its size, this big bug can fly, too.

- The dolphin is one of the world's fastest swimmers. Some dolphins can swim 40 miles an hour! Playful and friendly, the dolphin loves to swim alongside ships. And this great swimmer isn't even a fish. The dolphin is a mammal.

- Most animals have to spend a lot of time finding food and shelter, but parasites depend on other animals. Some dogs are experts on one of the best-known parasites—fleas!

FLEAS ?!!! HOW EMBARRASSING...

● When honeybees dance on the face of the honeycomb, it's not just for fun. They are really letting other bees from their hive know where to find food.

Fellow workers watch the honeybee dance and are able to get directions that will lead them to the exact location of the pollen and nectar.

● Many animals know how to do some things from the minute they're born. Fish are born knowing how to swim, and no one has to teach a spider how to build a web. This special knowledge an animal is born with is called instinct. Don't you wish you were born knowing how to do math problems?

THE PUFFER FISH

A "PUFFED-UP" PUFFER FISH

A PUFFER FISH AT NORMAL SIZE

● Some fish that live deep in the ocean have their own sources of light. These fish have special parts under their eyes that act like little light bulbs helping the fish see their way through the pitch-dark ocean. What are they called? Lantern-eye fish!

● Puffer fish look quite ordinary when they are swimming along. But when they are threatened by an enemy, they can expand to several times their normal size. Filled with water, the puffer fish look much bigger, and the enemy is frightened away.

◆ IN THE ◆
NEXT VOLUME

Have you ever wondered when the bicycle was invented, or if a car could fly, or which train is the fastest in the world? You can find these answers and lots more in volume 5, *Cars, Trains, and Other Wheels— Rolling Right Along*.